Beginners Vibe Guide

The Millennial Success Map
Walking in Purpose before Your 30's

Kay Johnson

Copyright © 2021 by Kay Johnson
Self-published Inspired Bosses, LLC / Amazon, LLC

Front Cover design Na'Deja Brantley | nbeearts.com
Photographer Alishia Zuniga | Cutting Images:Instagram and Facebook

Uploading or distributing photos, scans, or any content from this book without prior permission is theft of the author's intellectual property. Please honor the author's work as you would your own. Thank you in advance for respecting the author's rights.

All rights reserved. No part of this book may be reproduced or transmitted in any form or by any means without written permission from the author.

For permission requests, please contact the publisher at:
Inspired Bosses
support@beginnersvibeguide.com

For special orders, quantity sales, course adoptions and corporate sales, please email the publisher at support@beginnersvibeguide.com

Beginner's Vibe Guide: The Millennial Success Map
Walking in Purpose Before Your 30s

ASIN: B0956BFNBQ
ISBN: (print) 978-0-578-91259-2
BISAC category code: SELF-HELP / Entrepreneurship & Inspirational

Printed in the United States of America

615-593-6104

Table of Contents

Introduction... 1

My Beginning.. 3

Part 1: **Creating Yourself**

   Vibe #1: Vision............................... 13

   Vibe #2: Self-Love.......................... 17

   Vibe #3: Self-Acceptance 20

   Vibe #4: Self-Compassion 23

   Vibe #5: You Are the Light 25

Part 2: **Finding Yourself**

   Vibe #6: Self-Exploration 28

   Vibe #7: Self-Discovery 31

   Vibe #8: Self-Worth 34

   Vibe #9: Self-Confidence 37

   Vibe #10: You Are the Leader 40

Part 3: **Rules of Engagement**

> *Vibe #11*: Make Your Bed 45
>
> *Vibe #12*: Connect the Dots 51
>
> *Vibe #13:* No Compromise................55

Vibe #14: Don't Turn Down the Volume...61

Vibe #15: You Are the Vibe..............63

Acknowledgments..........................70

VIBE DEFINITION:

"a person who disrupts norms by walking in supernatural confidence"

Read what Leaders and CEOs are saying...

"Amazing perspective on the Leadership mantle, I absolutely love the story and relationship described with the leadership position.

One of the key takeaways in this story is the constant development of one's self. Leadership is character in motion, one with a servant mindset.

My takeaway is that when one accepts the responsibility of leadership they forfeit their own rights for the rights of those they have been blessed to serve."

Raymond Wright Sr., Wr*ight Way Coaching*

"If you are struggling with pains from your past or feel stuck in life and can use a guide, this is the ideal book to pick up! Kaylah overcame trials that has kept many people in arrested development well into their late 30's. The transparency that is shared in this book will make you feel that you are not alone and help you create the vibe you are looking for and deserve!"

~**Lionel Hilaire, Co-Founder of *Divine Potential Services and Author of Cultivate Your Calling***

"The Beginners Vibe Guide made me pause to focus on how I see myself. We allow our imaginations to be boxed in by the world around us and we lose the ability to see the potential of who we are called to be. Reading through the Vibes helped me to reconnect with God's vision for my life and quiet the lies of limitation. I am the Light. I AM THE VIBE!" - **Jeremy Perry, M.A Ed. | *Founder, Athletes Can | Author, Your Purpose is Your Platform***

Introduction

For as long as I can remember, I have always wanted to be perfect. When I think of myself as being perfect, I mean without blemish, shame, guilt, error, or fault.

As I started to write this introduction for you, I questioned my ability to reach you where you are. I wish I was perfect for so many reasons, but that is the one idea that keeps my words from forming chapters and my chapters from forming books.

I felt a growing urge inside my body and mind. You could almost address it as a "pull" or "tug". I have spent many hours training and learning. I have been studying what it means to be me in this world. So, right now, my only intention is to share my heart, my thoughts, and my world with you.

As I'm typing this, I think about how I am 24 years young and sitting in my mom's house in my hometown of Humboldt, Tennessee. Wow, what a start! I can honestly say, I never thought that this day would arrive.

After confronting fears, lies, depression, suicidal thoughts, failed platonic and romantic relationships, I am here, now. I would be remiss if I did not mention the greatest force, love, and strength in my life. You may know this love for yourself and, if you do not, please let me formally introduce you to the divine power and spirit

Beginner's Vibe Guide: The Millennial Success Map of God. God has always known me and He knew that you would pick up this book and read it, because you, muchlike me, need it.

As I end this introduction, I want to thank every person who has come into my life and shared their experiences with me... I wonder if my grandmother, Carrie Mae Johnson, knew my life would come to this? I miss her dearly...she has been the anchor to my soul during trying times. Joe Nathan Johnson, a man of great valor, I love you too as you still live in this year 2021. Thank God for the lineage I come from.

My Beginning...

The beginning is often the hardest part of your life to face because you had no "say so" in your being born. You didn't choose your parents, whether you have a good relationship with them or not. You did not choose your skin color, your height, the color of your eyes, the way your voice will sound when you speak, nor if you will be left-handed or right-handed.

In light of these choices that you did not have authority over, you were also not allowed to choose how your life starts. You were born a baby, innocent and unprepared for the life ahead of you. Do you ever look at your baby pictures and think to yourself, "Wow, I'm a little human in this photo! I wonder what I was smiling at or crying for." I've done this on numerous occasions.

When I look at my infant self, it reminds me of what I did not concern myself with before I became a young woman. My infant beginnings remind me of the love I had for my life and my world. Baby Kay was perfect in her mother's sight, but little did she know that she would spend 23 years trying to be perfect for everyone she knew.

Beginner's Vibe Guide: The Millennial Success Map

Because I had no choice in who I was born to, this left me in a place of certainty. I was certain that life was black and white. Life had not presented me with the grey areas. By the time I was two, I could understand American English language. Take a walk with me as I reminisce into my beginnings.

I was living on Craddock St. on the west side of Humboldt, TN in a small two-bedroom home with my mother and her then husband. Brian was the only man I knew to be my father. He fed me, protected me, clothed me, and cared for me.

Looking back, I can guess how much strength and courage it took my mom to make the changes she had to make. My mom is an optimistic, happy, bright, peaceful lady. She seeks to do no one any harm. If you look up the definition of sweetheart, you would see her face right there in the middle of the page. She is gentle, caring, thoughtful, forgetful, playful, energetic, nurturing, knowledgeable, empathetic, slow to anger, and a little ditzy at times. I love her more than you'll ever know. She is my primary source of reason and she will always be special to me. Mom, if you are reading this, don't cry, just embrace the moment because you deserve moments of joy for everything you gave me.

I can remember playing around in my room, doing what children do best-- using my imagination because, at that time, my brother Zion was not yet born. My mom, Charity, called me over to the phone and, even as a little girl, I got a sudden feeling that this could be a serious moment. I grabbed the phone with my beautiful wide-mouthed smile, showing all the teeth in my mouth. When you're a child and you get to talk on the phone, that is the best moment of your little life.

The moment had arrived! On the other side of the phone, two-year-old me heard this thundering, deep, dark, concerned, and surprising voice. "Was it your father?" Yep! You guessed it! That voice was my biological father, Travis.

My dad is tall, dark, outgoing, playful, caring, humorous, athletic, talented, observant, intelligent, strong, a firecracker, and a "no-nonsense" type of African American male from East St. Louis, Missouri.

This is my first recollection of him. His voice was powerful and that day he told me, "Kaylah, I'm your daddy."

My little two-year-old life was turned upside down and all around that night. From then on, I knew something there was special about my situation and people would call me special my entire twenty-four years of living.

Do you believe you are special? You have to because you are reading this guide and only special people like you know how to find the light in the darkness. Think about your upside down, turn-around moment, how did you respond and does it affect your life today?

It's kind of weird putting a two-year-old into a situation like that because now, in my little head, I'm thinking how the man in this house can't tell me when to go to bed anymore. Tehehehe! Little did I know that I would be spending twenty-two years searching for what I didn't receive from Travis in other men.

I learned that your father is the first man to love you and represents the standard of love you look for in a significant other. I was indirectly taught that daddies are meant to spoil you, be there for you, and protect you. If I am being honest, I always felt a little insecure in this area of my life because my daddy would always be 300+ miles away from me.

It wouldn't be until later that I find out why certain weeds are in our gardens. What do I mean by that? Keep reading.

I listened to a sermon once and the pastor gave this analogy about weeds in a garden. He referred to these weeds as challenges, struggles, pains, heartaches, and sufferings. The garden represents a good thing.

When you look out at a garden, you see the life of the vegetables, fruits, and plants. Think of your life as a garden. Weeds are one of those things the gardener tries to keep away but they always seem to pop up.

In light of the sermon, the revelation I received is that we all have weeds that grow in our garden and, sometimes, we have no control over them, but we can recognize them and pluck them out. I could've let this weed of not having my biological father present in my life paralyze me but, somehow, I reached heights that I know he's proud of.

The enemy will use the weeds to distract you, destroy you, kill you, and steal from you. Now, don't be afraid to keep reading because yes, these words are powerful, but you are **more** powerful!

The enemy comes to kill your purpose, destroy your life, steal your time and peace, and distract you from success.

What are the weeds in your life? I spent years searching for what I did not receive from Travis in romantic relationships. I was searching for security, safety, love, protection, vision, and assurance.

The funny thing about this search is that I have believed in God my entire life. I was raised in the church, so you would think that I knew where to find these comforts. I had so much to learn about God's sovereignty. I spent so much time looking for these things in the wrong places that I ended up with heartbreaks, failed relationships, fear of rejection, fear of abandonment, co-dependency issues, lack of proper self-worth, an improper vision of myself, and low confidence. I am healed and I walk in freedom!

Dr. Matthew Stevenson says, "It doesn't matter where you come from, but it matters where you come from." I believe that. Do you believe that? We all originated from somewhere and someone and that part matters for your destiny and your identity, but where you come from should not hinder or hold you back from what you are purposed to be.

Forgive.

Forgiveness is one of the toughest and most necessary acts we all must submit to in this life. Forgiveness is the gateway to a more joyful heart, brighter outlook on life, and sweeter tone to bear. Forgiving others grants access to the moments in life you need forgiveness for yourself. Forgive those who trespass against you and those you trespass against.

In this life, you will encounter moments where you must forgive yourself and other people who are closest to your heart. The only way someone can truly hurt us or cause pain in our life is by being so close to our heart and mind.

Forgive because you know one day you will not get it right.

Forgive because you know there is beauty that can be learned from "mistakes".

Forgive because you know life is too short to walk around being bitter, resentful, and unhappy.

Forgive because God forgives you.

POEM BY *Kay Johnson:*

You Are, So Be.

You are the light of the world if you allow yourself to be.

You are the dance to a rhythm if you let yourself be.

You are the smile on the face of another if you let yourself be.

You are the reason people laugh if you let yourself be.

You are the strength in someone's weak moment if you let yourself be.

You are the courage in her weak moments if you let yourself be.

You are the surprise in his day if you let yourself be.

You are the sweet stuff people can't get enough of, if you let yourself be.

Beginner's Vibe Guide: The Millennial Success Map

But see, we must submit to forgiveness
Because we all need a rainy day, a snowy day
Even when we want the rain to go away
Even if we could pray all the pain away
Just let yourself
Be.

Part 1: Creating Yourself

The wheel of life represents our life broken down into pie slices of energy, time, attention, and service. This is what I've used to walk in purpose before my 30s as well as align my life with supernatural timing and reason.

Beginner's Vibe Guide: The Millennial Success Map

Wheel of life

AREAS OF LIFE

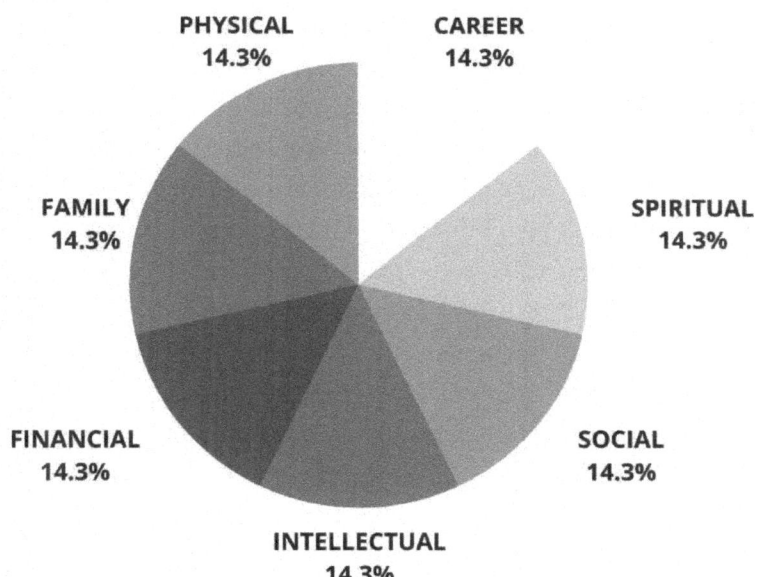

Inspired Bosses

Vibe #1: **Vision**

When I visualize my highest self, I think about my imagination, creativity, freedom, and limitless possibilities! The woman that I see in my mind has accomplished the plans of God for her life.

Vision is not about what you see daily in your earthly realm. When you allow your vision to sleep with you, eat with you, breathe with you, walk with you, sit at the table, and talk with you, then you're in alignment.

Children are the best at this because the world has not yet come crashing down on their imagination nor their limitless possibilities. Children are free to believe whatever they want, and nobody thinks twice about telling them they can't be a superhero.

If you saw someone yelling at a child, "NO, YOU WILL NEVER BE A SUPERHERO!" What would you think? The funny thing about this example is that we are screaming and repeating these exact words to ourselves day in and day out because the world has made us forcibly afraid to dream as children do.

No matter what, you must allow yourself to have vision. See the world in your child-like eyes and restore the love you once had for yourself.

Vision is less about the **"when"** and more about the freedom it gives you to write your own story.

I went through a period of my life where I lost vision. My sight was blurry and every day, it was as if I

Beginner's Vibe Guide: The Millennial Success Map woke up wearing three-week-old contact lenses. Because my vision for myself had been obscured and mishandled, I was unable to look at other people and see the beauty of life and creation.

Are you waking up every morning with three-week-old contact lenses on?

Are you allowing the world to rip your freedom and creativity away from you bit by bit?

Right now, while you read these words on this page, I want you to take a deep breath, close your eyes, and give yourself permission to dream about the one thing you wish you could be doing right now. For you, it may be sitting on a private island with the love of your life or playing board games with your family while everyone cracks jokes about one another. Whatever your utopia may be, I want you to go there.

The most powerful thing about you, a human being, is that we can go places we have never been before with the power of thought. If you are a visual thinker like me, your mind develops pictures as people describe a situation or even as I write this book.

I visualize you sitting down at the coffee table reading this book and highlighting your favorite vibes, gems, and ah-ha moments while people are ordering mochas lattes, and bagels.

Beginner's Vibe Guide: The Millennial Success Map

Our minds are a powerful tool and, if we allow ourselves to live without vision, we allow ourselves to live without our secret ingredients to living the life we once dreamt about as an energetic kid.

Sometimes we have to forgive ourselves for not exercising our ability to visualize the possibilities and settling for daily, average routines.

Vision can be restored with a little practice and relentless commitment. The commitment you have to make is with yourself. To do that, read the next sentence very slowly. **1…2….3 say "I commit to my vision _____."**

You fill in the blank. Be sure to write your vision or the date of your commitment to the vision and think of it as marrying your vision.

We don't always see ourselves properly, which is the reason I had to take those three-week-old contact lenses out of my eyes. I got extremely tired of walking around every day with unbelief, pinned up bitterness, wishing for certainty, and an average mindset.

Are you tired yet vibrating on a low vibe? I think so because you are reading this book and no matter your age, you are alive. Your being alive inspires me to believe that now you have the time to visualize a present or a future adding your child-like fearless faith.

Beginner's Vibe Guide: The Millennial Success Map

Here are a few scriptures to keep in mind when forming and holding on to your vision:

Daniel 2:19 AMP

"Then the secret was revealed to Daniel in a vision of the night, and Daniel blessed the God of heaven."

Hosea 12:10 NCV

"I spoke to the prophets and gave them many visions: through them, I taught my lessons to you."

Numbers 12:6 NCV

"He said, "Listen to my words: When prophets are among you, I, the LORD, will show myself to them in visions; I will

Habakkuk 2:2

"The Lord answered me: "Write down the vision; write it clearly on clay tablets so whoever reads it can run to tell others."

Vibe #2: Self-Love

Have you ever been around an infant when they experience seeing themselves in the mirror for the first time? One day in 2018, I was scrolling through my Instagram feed and there was this video of a baby standing in the mirror while the mom recorded this baby's interaction with herself. The baby only had a diaper on and I thought this was the ultimate moment for cuteness. In addition to this baby being so adorable, the baby was staring at herself and kissing herself while slobbing on the mirror. That baby was the utmost and deepest example of what self-love looks like. This was my "A-HA!" moment. In the caption, the mother wrote, "What real self-love looks like". It was at this moment that everything about self-love made sense.

I instantly went into reflection mode! This is the time when you ask yourself those deep dive questions to pull out the wisdom from your soul. For me, those questions were:

"When was the last time I fell in love with the woman in the mirror?"

"How did I get so comfortable with being rude and pessimistic with myself?"

"When was the last time I truly put myself at the **TOP** of my to-do list?"

Beginner's Vibe Guide: The Millennial Success Map

This baby has not begun to know the pressures of life or insidious and cruel thinking.

Where do I go from here because I didn't love me?

When I think of how I love or express love, it is through quality time and conversation. If you know the theory about the five love languages, then walk with me here.

Quality time is one of my top love languages and I was not even spending intentional quality time with the woman in the mirror. The woman in the mirror rarely got a chance to be kind to her reflection.

The other love language I cater to is words of affirmation. When I gently speak to other people, they can bet their bottom dollar that I am expressing my gratitude and love for who they are to me.

Although we all gravitate towards our preferred expressions of love, I realized that, to be a vibe and live a fulfilling life, I must express the love within to the woman in the mirror. I thought that my alone time and quiet time were wasted and inferior to being with others out and about.

When you realize that the time you spend with yourself is not wasted, you will unlock your greatness!

Make investments in yourself.

Kiss yourself in the mirror.

Take photos of yourself when you are at the pinnacle of joy.

Record the silly moments you wish to experience over and over again.

You are worth the moment, the experience, the love, and the time. You are the best investment to always sow into. If you don't pray for yourself, care for yourself and you live with you every day, how can someone else share love with you? Are you truly in LOVE with yourself?

It always hurt so bad to love myself the least, but now that I am done putting me last, my pain has taught me to love me first." - **Kay Johnson**

<u>Action step</u>: Say "I love you" to yourself every day for three weeks. Write it down, say it in the mirror, whisper it to yourself. Do whatever it takes for 90 days.

Vibe #3: Self-Acceptance

"Wanting to be someone else is a waste of the person you are".

- *Marilyn Monroe*

"The worst loneliness is to not be comfortable with yourself."

- *Mark Twain*

"If you stare at yourself long enough while in the mirror, you'll begin to realize and understand that you are all that is present. You are..."

"If you wonder what it's like to be in his or her shoes too often, your shoes may never get a chance to be worn. The world can't afford losing footsteps as rare as yours" **- Kay Johnson**

The frustrating part about who you are is facing what you have been through. We have all experienced turbulent times in our life that either forced us to grow or forced us to take a deeper look within.

One of the hardest things to do in my life was accepting all that I am. Accepting all that I am included, but was not limited to, my height, my family, my residence, my education, my experiences, my hair, the scars on my body, and everything that I deemed was a flaw about me. One thing we can learn from King David in his Psalms is that it is perfectly fine to be human and to express ourselves as human beings would. We have many colorful emotions that are the inner workings of a complex DNA.

Have you ever wanted to change your life in any way at all? Have you ever looked at television and thought to yourself, "man I wish...." and whatever follows allows you to escape your life for two seconds. Learn to get rid of the "I wish" mentality and work for your prosperity.

The bright side of self-acceptance is that you are very capable of living the life you spend all day and night pondering over. Are you willing to accept your situation and live your life? If you don't live your life, ask yourself this question-- who is directly or indirectly connected to me that may become a casualty?

You have no time to constantly compare yourself to wishes on a star that bear no weight in what you become. The world will never know who you truly are and all that you are capable of because you simply do not give yourself a fair chance. Vibe number three is easy to understand, yet more difficult to live out.

Take this as your strongest call to action. Embrace what is, forget what is not, let go of what was, and be grateful for what is to come.

Beginner's Vibe Guide: The Millennial Success Map

Your life ends the day you spend it attempting to live a "CC" or "copy and paste" version of those you admire or envy.

Action step: Write out five character traits that you absolutely love about yourself and share them with one person you trust.

Beginner's Vibe Guide: The Millennial Success Map

Vibe #4: Self-Compassion

When you are compassionate with yourself, you trust in your soul, which you let guide your life. Your soul knows the geography of your destiny better than you do."
- John O'Donnohue

To remain 'the vibe', you must learn to be compassionate with yourself. The inner you is much more deliberate, focused, wise, understanding, and aligned with the purpose of your life.

How do you begin to be compassionate?
When I think of compassion, I hear the words soft and gentle-- be soft and gentle to yourself with every move you make. You are living your life for the first time and no one has ever done this before. No one has ever been you before. Lighten up and enjoy the beauty of being a beginner. There's a blank canvas out there waiting for you to create your life and draw out your legacy.

"To be nobody but yourself in a world which is doing its best, night and day, to make you everybody else means to fight the hardest battle which any human being can fight; and never stop fighting."
- E.E. Cummings

"I found in my research that the biggest reason people aren't more self-compassionate is that they are afraid they'll become self-indulgent. They believe self-criticism is what keeps them in line. Most people have gotten it wrong because our culture says being hard on yourself is the way to be."
- Dr. Kristin Neff

Learning to be softer with the words we speak to ourselves in our heads is the same as being gentler to a newborn baby. We don't criticize the baby for crying because it knows no words to speak. We don't even think of harming the baby with harsh words because he/she poops on themselves. If we learn to speak to ourselves and treat ourselves if we were six days old again, our energy could alter the rooms we enter.

Choosing to be less critical of ourselves automatically returns the favor to those around us. They will notice your difference, your *inner-g,* and your trustworthiness. People can trust, but in most cases, we lack the desire. Why? We need more compassion and it starts with recognizing that we attract what is in us.

Action step: Be kind to yourself. Monitor your thoughts for 48 hours. Record your discoveries.

Vibe 5: **You Are the Light**

Choosing when and how to shine in any place is where I struggled the most. Lights come on and off, but somehow even in darkness, you can shine/see.

What is light? Light is an open space of appreciating vulnerability. Light expands across all geography. Light exposes what is hidden. Light is presence and power.

As a little girl, I would be afraid to walk around in the dark. Why? I was unable to see what was ahead of me, beside me, behind me, or around me. All that was visible or known was that I am me in the middle of this darkness. When you embrace your light, you understand that darkness cannot harm you. As a child, you may or may not have slept with a night light.

As I got older, I became more at peace with the darkness of a room and the stillness. Even now, as I write, I think of why light is important. We keep the bathroom light on so that it keeps the hallway lit enough for someone to pass through. What is the logic behind this action? People need to and want to know where they are stepping, headed, or what they are leaving behind.

All of the great people who have come before us were lights. If it weren't for their tenacity keeping the lights on for us in different spaces, light may not have existed. We don't injure ourselves. Right now, think of your greatest human inspirations. Mine are Oprah, Angela Davis, Myles Munroe, Cindy Trimm, Maya Angelou, and my grandmother, Carrie Mae.

Action step: Walk into a room and be dangerously kind without expecting anything in return. Be compassionate! Say hello to everyone who walks by and smile for no reason at all. Watch your attitude transform and the eyes of gratitude form.

Part 2: Finding Yourself

Immerse yourself in the Earth.
Immerse your soul into the universe. Become one with water, wind, fire, and earth.
You go outside of yourself into the Earth.
Become one with nature. Glide into purpose...

Vibe #6: Self-Exploration

Where have you journeyed?
Where have you been?
Where are you going?
When does this all come to an end?

I realize that I must give myself permission to travel one day. Contrary to popular belief, this was not the "normal" journey I'd take. This journey would cause me to dig into graves of my past. No one granted me permission to explore what I had produced on Earth.

What we must realize that, throughout our exploration phases of life, it is more likely we must take this journey alone. Your closest friend will not be able to walk with you as you dig deeper into your identity. Time and experiences have shaped your productivity. Explore the agreements and clauses you have committed to. These agreements and clauses are words and beliefs you subscribe to and believe in your heart.

Did you agree to spend your time in sorrow?

Did you sign a legally binding contract with your worries and fears?

Have you read over the fine print that proclaims defeat in your darkest hours?

Will you sign a lifelong lease that binds you to sickness, lack, and an impoverished mindset?

See, we must explore these clauses and agreements with more intention. Understand that these are the trails of seeds that are buried in fertile soil. This fertile soil is capable of reproducing ten times what's nurtured.

"Start with the end in mind." Stephen Covey. Wherever you find yourself on your journey, begin with your ending. Visualize your 102-year-old self. Are there words you never spoke, people you had no chance to meet, cities and countries your feet never stepped foot on...etc,?

"Your feelings are so important to write down, to capture, and to remember because today you're heartbroken, but tomorrow you'll be in love again." Anonymous

These are words I wrote in my "Remember the Journey" journal. Your thoughts and feelings become actions, your actions become habits, and your habits become who you are to everyone that exists in your life. Make no mistake in disowning the power of your journey. It is yours and you must realize the purpose of each facet of life you explore.

Action step: Explore what hurts you, what annoys you, what calms you, and what excites you. Get to know yourself on another level. Go deeper with you. Go try new food, go wear new clothes and hairstyles. Make new friends.

Beginner's Vibe Guide: The Millennial Success Map

Vibe #7: Self-Discovery

The power of a thought.

The timing and the silence of unpacking the ideas, beliefs, and emotions that have traveled deep within your soul.

The soul connects you to the universe, which was created and established by God, our Creator.

Did you know you are similar to God?

Is God a woman or man?

Does God care for you?

Are you the expression of what it means to be _____ ?

(insert your name here.)

I discovered that silence is sometimes my favorite hangout spot. Silence gives space for my wondering, my uncertainty, my certainties…It is the place where I allow myself to rest or race. As I write Vibe #7, I am experiencing a silence that is warm and cozy. This silence has created a conducive environment to write to the heart of the reader and the learner.

Are you just a reader?

Are you just a learner? I discovered the best version of my heart, mind, and soul.

"If you hear a voice within you say you cannot paint, then by all means paint and that voice will be silenced." Vincent VanGogh

Beginner's Vibe Guide: The Millennial Success Map

Our fears, worries, doubts, and insecurities all carry a sound of conviction with them. It is your conscious decision to agree or disagree with the words they speak.

"Sometimes you wake up, sometimes the fall kills you. And sometimes, when you fall, you FLY." - Neil Gaiman

When you discover certain vices, habits, and beliefs about yourself, you may sink into a low place and think to yourself: "I hate this about me, I wish this could change, this can't be true, or my favorite... wow, is this really who I've been?"

Recognize. Respect. Accept.

Recognize your moments of frustration and ease.
Respect the emotions that are stirred beyond your approval.
Accept that you can change your decisions, which ultimately change your actions, then spill over into your character.
Everything about what you want and need is unveiled one day at a time. If you are like me, there are times when you want everything NOW. Other times, you come to realize that you don't even need what you're desiring. Most times, you find tiny pockets of gratitude

that come with the realization that appreciating your now is the only real guarantee in life.

<u>Action step:</u> Take a solo trip. Take a day trip. Go to the lake, river, mountain, or beach alone. Drive the car you've always wanted to drive. Give yourself permission to see that thing you've always wanted to see. Take yourself on an outing. Write about it in your journal or share it with someone else. Now, plan the next one!

Beginner's Vibe Guide: The Millennial Success Map
Vibe #8: Self-Worth

Start writing, "I love you" letters to yourself and watch your life transform.

I began to write "I love you" letters to myself around August 2018. I started seeing that I was worthy of love and needed to love myself.

Worth is about affirming yourself before others have the opportunity to build you up or break you down. The paradigm shift my life underwent after applying the principles of affirmations would not have been possible had I not learned to affirm myself. This paradigm shift set the tone for my entrepreneurial journey.

There is one thing you must realize and that is-- your thoughts become you. Here's one actionable step you can take to turn your vibe into reality.

Wake up, look yourself in the eyes, speak with clarity and say, "I am worthy of all good opportunities, I love you, _____ (**insert your name**).

"What has transpired that shifted the trajectory of your life?"

WORTHY AFFIRMATIONS:

No matter the challenges I face, I am worthy of victory.

No matter how many people leave me, I am worthy of being kept.

No matter how many times I misunderstand, I am worthy of understanding.

No matter how many people call me special or different, I am worthy of admiration.

No matter what punches life throws at me, I am worthy of a resilient comeback season.

WORTHY THOUGHTS:
Proverbs 23:7 KJV

"For as he thinketh in his heart, so is he: Eat and drink, saith he to thee; but his heart is not with thee".

As you begin to speak these words into your life over and over again, you must be sure your heart matches your words. Most times, we speak and take action without our heart's consent or approval. Your thoughts attract actions and this is why you receive a certain result when you speak to a certain situation. However, only the heart attracts what it is truly prepared for.

Your heart is prepared in moments that you believe come to break you.

Your heart is prepared when the pieces seem to have fallen on the floor.

Beginner's Vibe Guide: The Millennial Success Map

Your heart is prepared when you surrender your control.

Now is the time to schedule your appointment for *coronary artery bypass grafting* (open heart surgery).

Remodeling self-worth encompasses the work of the surgeon and the surrender of the patient. Once this process is in motion and complete, the healing begins. Our wounds of self-hatred and self-criticism become battle scars and reminders of the fight towards destiny and purpose.

Action step: Write I love you letters to yourself. Don't wait on the love of your life to show up, don't wait on your parents or anyone in your family to tell you. Tell yourself for 90 days.

Vibe #9: Self-Confidence

Committing to the plan, the choice, and the misstep even when it constitutes feelings of fear and second-guessing is hard. Confidence is the deal-breaker. Confidence is the secret vibe that changes the trajectory of your future. Confidence means being reliant on your innate abilities to achieve.

In high school, I participated in the Miss Black Gibson County Scholarship Pageant, a county-wide scholarship pageant. 2013 would be my first time competing in such a 'girly' activity since leaving middle school.. I grew up with boys. I was a basketball player who enjoyed wearing sneakers, shorts, and slouching every chance I could get.

This competition put me out of my comfort zone for sure. There were four pageant categories for the scholarship: fundraising, interview, talent, and evening gown. I was sixteen years old and knew nothing about interviewing or fundraising on a local nor large scale.

The first year I participated in the pageant, I failed miserably with a mediocre score. My confidence plummeted and this was fact-based evidence/fuel I could use to convince my mother that I should not be competing in activities such as this. My mother had other goals in mind.

She needed me to have some extra funds for college, so she challenged me to compete again. She was right about the college funds. Although I worked extremely hard to win, I did not.

After this, it was time for self-reflection and execution. My aunts, Christina and Angela, were so convincing as the new year rolled around to compete. There I was again, competing for the title of Miss Black Gibson County 2014.

I analyzed all that I was penalized for in the first year and made it my mission to improve and walk away with the crown.

As I was preparing to be crowned, I recalled a moment where I did not believe in myself or my ability to improve. Carrie Mae, my grandmother, came to the rescue.

My grandmother sat with me, teaching me a valuable lesson that I will never forget. I want to share it with you.

Carrie Mae sat beside me on my mother's burnt orange sofa and picked up the remote control to the television. She explained to me that the remote control was something I owned, and every button was controlled by me. I listened intently while watching her carefully. She was always full of surprise 'gems'. Carrie Mae said to me, "Anytime you get ready, remember you have control of what happens, if you want to turn on your confidence just press the button."

Needless to say, I was crowned Miss Black Gibson County 2014 with an almost perfect score of 99 out of 100. The remote control was the trigger!

It was at that moment I realized I was always confident, but the disconnect was my realization of the authority and control I possessed. The ultimate barrier to my success in confidence was the inability to accept the authority of my capabilities. I was always capable and the response to my abilities was a complete and utter achievement. This was one of the biggest years for MBGC (Miss Black Gibson County), its 20th anniversary, and as Queen, I earned the title and $4,000 toward my future endeavors.

Responsibility broken down means to *RESPOND TO YOUR ABILITIES*. Will you respond?

Action step: Take the remote and turn on your confidence. Practice confidence every day in at least one area of your life.

Beginner's Vibe Guide: The Millennial Success Map

Vibe #10: **You Are the Leader**

Your tribe, your audience, your followers--the people who are assigned to benefit and prosper from your life will show up. Frankly, some of them have already found their way into your circle of influence. What you must believe about yourself is, "You are the leader."

Leadership is not always beautiful. Leadership is about "being" an example, going first, and failing forward.

Do you desire leadership? Here are three questions to think deeply about.

How do you gain someone's trust to lead them?
Are leaders born or developed?
What is the price of leadership?

It was a freezing November day when I realized that leadership started with me, in my bedroom. The year is now 2017 and life has started to make more sense. It dawned on me that leadership was something I had danced with for almost my entire life. Well... at least when I started grade school.

Leadership roles were not always something I asked for; however, there were many times when leadership and I danced in harmony and yes, I led the way. Leadership and I would have conversations about when to speak, listen, or just take charge of the current situations we were experiencing. Leadership was like my closest friend growing up. Leadership went into every classroom with me from my elementary days onto my adult life.

Leadership and I were tight-- so tight we would argue when leadership wanted to pursue scholarship opportunities, stand up for individuals who were getting bullied at school, and even run for class president in the eleventh grade. Let me be the first to tell you, my leadership friend was very ambitious.

I would break up with leadership ever so often because, to be frank, I was tired of "eyes" being on me and the judgment of every person who wouldn't step to the plate lingering in my head. Thoughts like, "I could've done this better, said this more tactfully,etc.". You know, those usual self-criticizing thoughts we all have at times.

I would sit in a room with leadership and it would nudge me to volunteer for a position, but I would just sit there and look at leadership and say, "Uh uh, not today". Leadership never got tired of me, and I did not understand why at times. Did leadership take a liking to me because I was the granddaughter of a local hometown pastor, or because my mother was a local Gibson county school teacher?

Beginner's Vibe Guide: The Millennial Success Map

Leadership wants you to know that the dance is not always a smooth one where you both know the steps or groove to the beat with no skips or missteps, but you should lead anyway. Lead in tough times, hard times, great times, sad times, joyful times, painful times, and most of all, doubtful times.

It is important to lead from the back. Leadership, in my opinion, is always about putting others first, serving on another level, and listening to those who trust you enough to speak with you and follow you. There are many leaders, industries, homes, schools, and people, but there is only one you. How will you lead?

Do you remember those questions I asked at the beginning of this story? Here are some truths that leadership and I uncovered together.

It is possible to gain someone's trust to lead them. When you listen carefully and make space for their voice, you invite change. Leaders are born and have to be developed throughout life. It is not easy, nor is it for the faint of heart, but it is so worth the change we see in our lives and our nation.

I hope that you are not apathetic when it comes to the leadership role you are in, but that you are empowered while you listen and pay the price of leadership. This price has no numeric value, but the price you pay will develop your character and the world around you. So, lead!

Lead with compassion, a servant's mindset, and heart, and embrace the leader within.

Action step: Watch Simon Sinek's video on YouTube leadership. Identify your leadership style and tone. Surround yourself--ears, eyes, heart, mind-- with leaders that pull the best out of you. These could be people who are your best friends, or those who bring out the best in you. John Mason taught me this idea.

Part 3: **Rules of Engagement**

*Your **law**. Your interactions, operations, functions, logistics, strategies, plans, calendars, dates, thought patterns, and codes you live by.*

Vibe #11: **Make Your Bed**

Did you make your bed this morning? What's important about making your bed?

Making Your Bed plays a significant role in your success. Most of us are not pursuing significance, but status. I learned that status was a short way to say: '*still too arrogant to understand significance*'. It wasn't until I hit a brick wall that I learned that success was hidden in the vibe I create when I arise from bed. Significant people who maintain a morning and evening routine can verify that success is hidden in the small moments of life that most people do not glorify. We want to believe that success is all about the money we accumulate, the awards, and the materials that make us "look good".

The principal idea here is that, to be trusted with more, you will be tested to take care of little. When you get out of your bed, you are declaring your authority as soon as your feet hit the floor. You are saying to the world, your enemies, the attacks, the sorrow, the pain that; "I am here today!"

If you don't wake up in the morning with purpose, intention, and gratitude on your mind, someone who is attached to your purpose will become a casualty. If there is no realization of the authority you possess; with every step you make, the effect is the casualty of another. You are now released from the "*comfortable*" state of life.

Beginner's Vibe Guide: The Millennial Success Map

Making Your Bed requires a certain level of emotional intelligence. Our beds represent a state of being, comfortable and at rest. It is most important to remind yourself to wake up with intention.

Here is my *personal **"Make Your Bed"** Routine:*

1. Arise.
2. Check the time.
3. Look to the ceiling and thank God I'm alive.
4. Lay and connect to God's vision for my life.
5. Read a scripture verse, usually from NIV, NCV, AMP, and KJV versions of the Bible, or read a book of my choice.
6. Meditate—this allows me to organize my thoughts, think about who I want to be, assess my moods, and recall dreams or downloads God has completed throughout the night. Something like an iOS update for iPhone.
7. Smile and stretch-- this promotes joy and gratitude for the day and my life.
8. Pray, even if it's the Lord's Prayer or I take 30-45 minutes to kneel before God (sometimes more).
9. Check the weather and news.
10. Listen to podcasts, YouTube, or myself--These vary as I make time for raw and original input from God to me.

Beginner's Vibe Guide: The Millennial Success Map

11. Check my high-performance planners completed the night before.
12. Hygiene and attire-- attire is picked out the night before.
13. Read texts, emails & social media.
14. Drink water, take supplements/ vitamins and make breakfast, which is sometimes very quick and small.
15. Say good mornings and good days to people I love. I occasionally send encouraging texts to a person of my choice.

My day is ready to be won! Why are these fifteen steps important?

They help me to unlock supernatural vision, creativity, and confidence. At some point in your life, you must graduate from the pain that keeps you arrested in mediocrity. There is a mentality of "I just don't play about me anymore", that has to come into play sooner than later.

Your destiny is **NOT** a side hustle.

Your wins start small, you count them, and **YOU** make them count.

I believe three phases push you into operating on your highest frequency. Let's map it out.

Phase 1- Pit stop at pain: Here are the questions you must answer to understand your prayer and pain points.
1. What is important to me?
2. Who are my parents and others in my family tree?
3. What circumstances was I born into?
4. How have I reacted to my pain?
5. What can I not change about my life?
6. Who can I forgive without hearing their apology?
7. What has my pain taught me, molded me into?

Phase 2- Turn here at pandemic:

Internal pandemic is a reality that I had come to face. Before COVID-19 shut the world down and drastically changed millions of peoples' lives, I believe individuals were already suffering from inescapable realities that seem to have no happy ending. This phase is all about realizing freedom exist. Here you will perform the necessary work to eventually become best friends with FREEDOM. This is your game now. During physical therapy the only way the athlete is able to return to the game is because of his or her willingness to fight through the pain of the new fear, while breaking down the barriers of old fear. You are now re-establishing and rebuilding strength. This takes your full attention and

Beginner's Vibe Guide: The Millennial Success Map will become priority because you are accepting your role as authority. As you are in this phase there will be moments of weakness, discouragement, and disbelief. Your main job is to stay the course. You are not alone but you must take full responsibility for where you are now and where you are going. It's your journey, but most importantly, it is YOUR life.

Phase 3 - ETA: At the right moment and season of life you will arrive at clarity. Don't overthink your arrival. Spend time cultivating your spirit, heart, and mind. You have been through physical therapy and you have established a newer version of you. You may have found yourself stuck in previous phases or vibes of this book, and that's because it's not the end all be all. This is a Beginners Guide and the most beautiful aspect of being a beginner is that NO ONE expects you to be perfect on your first try. Remember, you are living your conscious reality for the first time. You are great at being you. The higher you knows, there is no lack, limits, or defeat. This you only knows VICTORY. Victory comes with a cost. What are you willing to put on the line for the greater you to break through? Know who you are. Know what you stand on. Know who you stand for. Know where you stand. Be courageous, this path is not crowded. Rare is uncommon. This game is NOT for the weak.

Action step: Take 2-3 weeks to explore the answers to these questions. Please know that it takes patience and understanding with ones' self.

Beginner's Vibe Guide: The Millennial Success Map

Vibe #12: **Connect the Dots**

"You can't connect the dots looking forward; you can only connect them looking backward. So you have to trust that the dots will somehow connect in your future." - Steve Jobs

This thought was transformational in building the confidence needed to share my story. Connect the dots of your pain and history. This is the place where you can be transformed and walk into freedom. Here's an excerpt from a poem by Marrian Williamson that continually reminds me of who I am.

Our Deepest Fear
"... It's not just in some of us; It's in everyone.
And as we let our own light shine,
We unconsciously give other people permission to do the same.
As we're liberated from our own fear,
Our presence automatically liberates others."

What does this mean for you? There is no one more special or important than you, but you must realize that now. We are special because we use our gifts and talents. Once you can understand what your pain is meant for, you can understand why you were born into a time such as this. The date you were born, where you were born, the hour of your birth, and the family you were born to all play a major role in your existence.

If you do not have a healthy relationship with someone in your family or your past, have you taken a deeper look into the soul of the complication? Look, the truth is, you are NOT the only person hurting or running from agony and affliction. It's time to stop dead in your tracks and face those skeletons in the closet. You do not have to do this alone! Here's what I did.

After experiencing a season of depression, I attempted to commit suicide. Yes, suicide. I believed that I should no longer be here on Earth and that somehow the world would be better off without me.

After this experience, I enrolled in therapy on my college campus. This was my last full year of college and it seemed like a disaster waiting to turn into a rainbow. The initial consultation was all about me.

Was I intending to harm myself?

Did I have intentions of harming someone else?

They wanted to be sure I was okay. This moment in my life was frightening. I did not seem like myself-- this was odd. Who I was becoming was incompatible with the woman I had always been.

When I try to explain what was going through my mind at the time, it is always extremely tough to describe how naked life was for me in that season. My brain was open, but it seemed like God had stripped me of all of the self-hatred and self-sabotage.

I was naked.

Nobody else could see or sense this nakedness. My nakedness was only something God and I could fix, but I had to be willing to submit to His plans of prosperity for my life.

Are you naked and afraid? You may not believe in taking this step toward healing and freedom, but I want to share this with you.

Remember this.

1. You are the only person who can rescue you.
2. You deserve a great life.
3. You are the sole proprietor of your life's story.
4. No one can make you feel like a mistake unless you grant them permission.
5. You know your pain better than anyone else, so do something about it.

Action step:

Write out what will happen if you do not take the step, whatever that step may be. Create a mind map. Here is a picture of my mind map.

Beginner's Vibe Guide: The Millennial Success Map

DOT CONNECTOR
MIND MAP

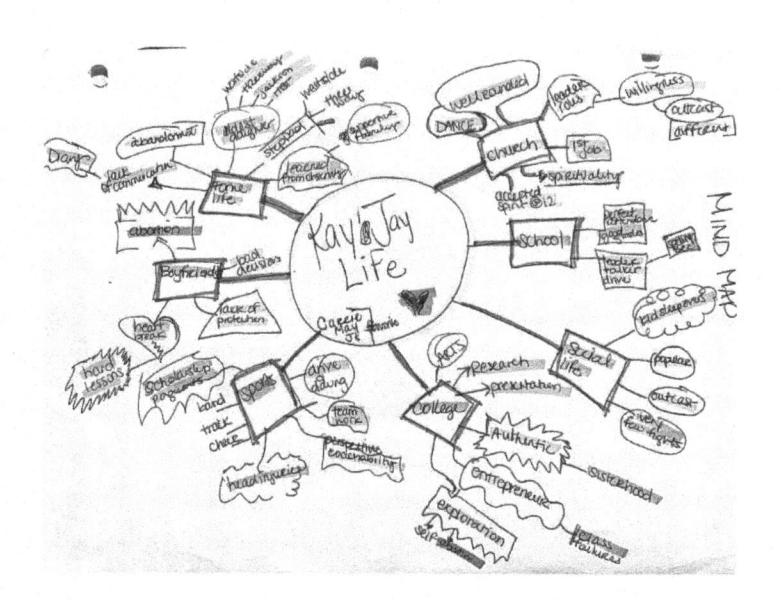

Vibe #13: **No Compromise**

In the Cambridge Dictionary online, compromise as a verb is defined as "to allow your principles to be less strong or your standards or morals to be lower." How often do you compromise your thoughts and beliefs for the sake of others "being okay"? I've spent a lot of time in this space.

In past relationships, compromising my beliefs became a perpetual cycle. I believed the other person was more important than I was. I had no real ownership of my personhood. There was a lack of belief about who I was. Here is a list of unwanted and discarded beliefs shaped during this phase of my life.

"I shouldn't say this because…."
"I'll just let them do it since they are…"
"She must be more….than me"

These were some deeply perverted thoughts that led to me always bending over backward for other people, never truly standing up for who I knew I was.

Have you ever been there before?

Are these fears and unwanted thoughts?

Do these fears and thoughts QUALIFY for where you are going in life?

We compromise what we believe because, when someone who appears very confident in what they believe shows up, we have second thoughts about what was original for us. We also do this because we want to be accepted and understood by everyone.

Do you know what compromise looks like? No boundaries! When we do not apply healthy boundaries in all situations, we tend to pay the cost after the action. We can't take what happened back, we can only own our decisions.

Every decision I made landed me in a relationship with someone who did not truly want to understand me. That is not the right vibe, so work on shifting out of that!

Action step: Answer the following questions.
1. Who am I?
2. Where am I from?
3. Why am I here?
4. What can I do?
5. Where am I going?

How to NOT compromise.

1. Become grounded in pragmatic principles that catapult your success and communicate those to people close to you.
2. Choose environments and people who choose you.
3. Check yourself regularly. Check your actions and words.
4. Be certain about what you bring to the table of resources and opportunity.
5. KNOW when to speak and KNOW when to listen.
6. Process the timing of all productivity.

Learn to fight and win

"If you know the enemy and know yourself, you need not fear the result of a hundred battles. If you know yourself and not the enemy, for every victory gained you will also suffer a defeat. If you know neither the enemy nor yourself, you will succumb in every battle."

Sun Tzu, *Art of War*

Here is my translation of this quote.

"Know yourself and know your enemy, you will always win.

If you know yourself but not know your enemy, for every victory gained you will suffer a loss.

If you neither know yourself nor your enemy, you will always lose."

One day, a fellow entrepreneur and I were discussing many different ideas and getting to know each other better and he said this, "I had to start to look at myself as my enemy would. If I were my enemy and I was the target, where would I hit? It's like an out-of-body experience. Kay, imagine you are a target and someone is attempting to bring you down and destroy you. Where would you aim, what would your attempt be—to distract, destroy, or delay your greatness?"

From there, we went on to discuss the process of triumph and defeat. There is indeed a force working against you. It is your duty to identify HOW that force will suffer defeat by the strength of your arm and your mountain-moving faith. Godly wisdom reveals to us that we all will be tested. The bible says you have the victory.

Proverbs 24:6 AMP
"For by wise guidance you can wage your war, And in an abundance of [wise] counselors there is victory *and* safety."

The scripture above is attached to the vision board I created in 2018.

Deuteronomy 20:3, 4 AMP

"And shall say to them, 'Hear, O Israel: you are advancing today to battle against your enemies. Do not lack courage. Do not be afraid or panic, or tremble [in terror] before them, 4 for the Lord your God is He who goes with you, to fight for you against your enemies, to save you.'

You do not lose when you are with and in God. On the flip side of that, you must not abuse God's grace and mercy on your life for situations you repeatedly rebel against. In God, there is safety and He does correct our behavior. This correction comes from love and, as I write this, I remember thinking and feeling as if God hates me when he corrects me.

So many of the ideas we have of God come from this human experience. We know that another persons' love and grace for us can be conditional and we stoop to the level of thinking that God is one and the same. God will indeed do whatever it takes to ensure one sheep's safety even if that means protecting the ninety-nine from a distance.

Will you be loyal to God like He's loyal to you?

Will you have the same faith in God that He had when created you in your mother's womb?

There is a divine potential in you and you must be the one to live it fully. Your grandparents didn't do it, your parents didn't do it… and that leaves you. God is not concerned with your materials from this existing world. God wants you to WIN.

My thought is that God is more concerned with HOW you win your battles. God wants you to win your battles with HIM as your source of strength. The character of a woman/man is tested through trials and tribulations.

What is built in you when you face adversity comes out of you when you walk in freedom, your winning season. I challenge you to be loyal to God and loyal to your purpose.

Vibe #14: Don't Turn Down the Volume

Spending lots of time turning down my volume in life made me feel as if people were continually trying to keep me mute.

As a kid in elementary school, I would get "T" for talking written in my agenda book daily. I hated bringing the agenda book home because I knew my mother would side with the teachers because, after all, she is an educator. It seemed as if talking was one of the worst things to do as a child. People always told you to "be quiet", "you're just a kid", and they would brush you off and, sometimes, for a good reason.

Getting those "T's" was something I didn't quite understand because I loved conversing with people. As a young kid, how would I know that people actually got paid for talking-- large quantities at that? In my young mind, this was the one activity that resulted in an undesirable disciplinary consequence.

Why would I ever in my life want to speak after years of getting into trouble and corrected for it? I love to talk! I love to hear my voice because it's unique and I don't sound like other people. I like to sing and express myself through writing and poetry.

Small instances such as this can grow into major roadblocks to targeting your gift.

Beginner's Vibe Guide: The Millennial Success Map

Remember these things: Here is your chance to write to your future self who unapologetically shows up in the world. Write whatever you feel.

Beginner's Vibe Guide: The Millennial Success Map
Vibe #15: **You Are the Vibe**

What does it mean for one to be a *"vibe"*? Repeat after me.

"I" ..." "AM" ... "THE" ... "VIBE".

When you walk into the room, it is now time to shift the atmosphere! You are now the thermostat. Thermostats are the devices that regulate the temperature of an enclosed space. Instead of adjusting to the temperature or the atmosphere of the room, let everyone in the room sense the upgrade when you enter. You have two ears and one mouth, meaning that there is not always a need to speak for attention. My Dad always says, "some people just got it like that." He's right-- some people balance speaking and listening better than others. Your weapon is your ability to be sensitive to a rooms' needs. People are listening to you, watching you, and waiting for you in these rooms.

As a 2021 Leader School graduate-- shout out to Dr. Matthew Stevenson of the All Nations Worship Assembly-- I learned that we must be sensitive to what is happening around us. Show respect in rooms that are not our normal and display the character that's being developed in us.

He also taught that we should lend some consideration to this idea-- you don't know everyone you're going to impact everywhere you're about to go. Therefore, you need to pick up on skills, reactions, responses, and adaptive behaviors. If you watch the right room with the right people, this will happen for you. Dr. Stevenson admonishes us to know that someone in some room will have the power to create a new door for you. This person will have the right access, information, and resources to increase your influence, so be careful to NEVER DISHONOR the room.

It's time to turn pain into power! After the pandemic, your pain can be birthed into purpose. Be careful of who you allow in your delivery room. Be very specific and protective of your birthright in God's Kingdom. God has an intention for you and the reason He chose for you to be born during times like these is that you have the capability of shifting the paradigm if you stay connected to His vine.

See, without God, I can do nothing. That's my belief. This book has been written in supernatural confidence and divine power. The contents of this book are sealed with truths that have shaped my life.

Don't ever force your importance in someone else's life! Know that you belong and, if there are no openings, create your own space and be sure to include the people and causes you care most about.

Learn to qualify and categorize fear.

Make a list of your fears and answer the questions that burden you most.

Fears are rooted deeply in our belief systems intertwined with judgment, religious practice, and experiences. How you feel about yourself and your life will determine what rooms you enter and how you set the tone.

As you experience this transformation, know that, as the process reveals your true identity, you will lose certain parts of you that no longer fit God's description for your future. People will be left behind, habits will be broken, thoughts will no longer seduce you, the pain will begin to show itself useful while healing and freedom become your portion.

"Don't let loyalty stagnate you or make you not communicate; loyalty does not mean I stay around or function in the same way -- if I end a relationship." Dr. Matthew Stevenson

You are now part of "THEE VIBE MASTER TRIBE".

Say this with me:

We use our pain to break through the barriers of discomfort and deceit.

We trust our gut feeling, which is a Godly feeling.

We look ahead with our eyes toward freedom.

Beginner's Vibe Guide: The Millennial Success Map

We disrupt norms by standing in power.
We no longer accept shame, guilt, and defeat as true.
We KNOW who we are.

We KNOW why we are.
We KNOW that no weapon formed against us shall prosper.

Give yourself permission today. Sign your name on the dotted line of success. Put your initials by strength and faith. Stamp the date of your arrival to purpose, it is here.

ACTION STEP BELOW:

I _____ (fill in your name), give myself permission to _____ _____ (fill in your dreams, purpose, intent, desires) and on this _____ (day/date/time), I embrace my next level of strength and faith. _____ (initials)

CRACK THE CODE OF PURPOSE

Dream build
Book the first-class flight
Visit the 1.1-million-dollar neighborhood
Talk to people who know nothing about you
Go test drive the life you want to design!
Invest in the $1,000 course
Fast for a year
Cut the person off
Change your hair
Express your feelings
Leave the job
Stop smoking the marijuana
Put the alcohol down
Pray for thirty minutes
Take a solo trip
Make sure you smile
Exercise 2-3 times a week
Allocate your finances
Taste the new food
Write down your wildest dream
Make a bucket list
Make new friends
Apply for the new position
Take notes on how to love yourself more intensely
Share your dreams with people that love you back

Write the book
Start the side hustle (your destiny isn't your side job though)
Make new friends everywhere you go
Get your haircut a different way
Laugh often
Write down your values
Trust your journey
Live your life…
After all, it is YOUR life.

YOUR PURPOSE HAS TO BECOME A NON-NEGOTIABLE IN YOUR LIFE. DON'T BREAK YOUR CONTRACT WITH PURPOSE.
YOU MAY BEND AND YOU MAY GET SCARRED, BUT
LET YOUR PURPOSE PREVAIL!

Beginner's Vibe Guide: The Millennial Success Map

VIBE TRACKER
FILTER FOR LIFE

WRITE OUT EVERYTHING IMPORTANT TO YOU

Self Image increases

Build Empire
VALUES
More Joy
THINGS NOT TO DO
WHAT'S IMPORTANT
Challenge Myself
New Story
Time Budget
Consistency key

Strong routine developed

Inspired Bosses

Acknowledgments

Lionel Hilaire
Tammie Polk
John Mason
Kimberly Taylor
Nadeja Brantley

Thank You

Brandi Cox
Kenneth Dunn
Kimberly Bryant
Marcus Branch
LaToya Tyus
Necole Jones
Lakesha Smith
Aijalon Payne
Lionel Hilaire
Brenda Duckett
Melissa Johnson
Tydarius Tyson
Deswick Bonds Jr.
Quantarius Webb
Charity Shepherd
Kennedy Washington
Carla Brown
Keturah Shelton

Thank You

Marcus Rogers
Delilah Hicks
Jenesis Anderson
Alayshia Clark
Cilisha Harper
Christina White
Whitney McCollins

SPONSORS

Tameko Toliver

Armond Webb

Meka Eguekwe

Frankie & Derek Johnson

Quantarius Webb

About the Author

Kaylah Johnson, also known as ***Kay***, is an energy force to be reckoned with. She is a professional Transition Specialist for the state of Tennessee, Leader School graduate and holds a Bachelor of Science degree in Health Sciences and Non-Profit Management.

Kay is the owner of Inspired Bosses, a business movement dedicated to guiding young minority girls and single millennial women into supernatural confidence through transformational and empowerment storytelling.

Kay is a proud recipient of the National Society of Leadership Success. She's worked as a beauty career counselor, clinical lead for the state of Tennessee, Shelby County District Attorney General office mentor, teacher assistant and activity coordinator.

In the arena of confidence, she immersed herself into the local and national modeling industry, traveling to Hollywood, California to work with ***America's Next Top Model*** winner, ***Laura James*** (cycle 19) and contestant ***Brittany Sharuan*** (cycle 11). As ***Kay*** volunteered her time and energy to *Harlem's Fashion Row* with founder ***Brandice Daniel***, she understood the importance of commitment to vision.

Misa Hylton, American stylist and fashion designer reminded ***Kay*** to "always go after her dreams and take the limitations off."

Julee Wilson, beauty director of the *Cosmopolitan*, advised her to always be "bold and different."

Kay has been featured on NBC/WNBJ Jackson, Tennessee news for the 83rd Annual West TN Strawberry Festival. In 2020, she hosted a national virtual health, wellness, and personal development summit during the height of COVID-19. ***Kaylah*** devoted her expertise to five minority women entrepreneurs through developing a pilot program for business and self-development.

Training middle school-aged minority girls on the importance of femininity and womanhood is one of Inspired Bosses' ways of moving the next generation forward.

Kaylah loves educating her students on the strategies of transitioning into the "real word". She admonishes them to be original and have fun while doing it.

Find out more about ***Kay*** at
www.inspiredbosses.com
www.beginnersvibeguide.com

Made in USA - North Chelmsford, MA
1309855_9780578912592
03.29.2022 0912